WILD NATURE

EXTREME ANIMALS

Steve Parker

Miles Kelly

First published as *My Top 20 Extreme Animals* in 2010 by Miles Kelly Publishing Ltd
Harding's Barn, Bardfield End Green, Thaxted, Essex, CM6 3PX, UK

Copyright © Miles Kelly Publishing Ltd 2010

This edition published in 2014

10 9 8 7 6 5 4 3 2 1

Publishing Director Belinda Gallagher
Creative Director Jo Cowan
Editorial Director Rosie Neave
Senior Editor Claire Philip
Concept Designer Simon Lee
Volume Designer Simon Lee, Rob Hale
Image Manager Liberty Newton
Production Manager Elizabeth Collins
Reprographics Stephan Davis, Thom Allaway
Assets Lorraine King

ISBN 978-1-78209-499-9

Printed in China

British Library Cataloguing-in-Publication Data
A catalogue record for this book is available from the British Library

ACKNOWLEDGEMENTS
The publishers would like to thank the following sources for the use of their photographs:
Key: (m) = main (i) = inset

Front cover: Winfried Wisniewski/Foto Natura, (Wild Nature animal globe) ranker/Shutterstock.com
Back cover: (top), Christian Musat/Shutterstock.com, (bottom) Holly Kuchera/Shutterstock.com
Page 1 belizar/Shutterstock.com
Pages 4–5 (clockwise from top left) John Mitchell/Photolibrary.com, Reinhard Dirscherl/Photolibrary.com,
Fritz Pölking/Photolibrary.com, Pete Oxford/naturepl.com, Nigel Dennis/Photolibrary.com
Sailfish (m) Doug Perrine/naturepl.com, (i) Doug Perrine/naturepl.com
Giraffe (m) Martin Harvey/Corbis, (i) Frans Lanting/FLPA
Peregrine falcon (m) Imagebroker/FLPA, (i) Mark Payne-Gill/naturepl.com
Elephant seal (m) Flip Nicklin/Minden Pictures/FLPA, (i) Ingo Arndt/naturepl.com
Black-throated hummingbird (m) Kim Taylor/naturepl.com, (i) Tom Vezo/naturepl.com
Stonefish (m) Georgette Douwma/naturepl.com
Sunfish (m) Hiroya Minakuchi/Minden Pictures/FLPA
Emperor penguin (m) Fritz Poelking/Photolibrary.com, (i) Rob Reijnen/Minden Pictures/FLPA
Army ant (m) Piotr Naskrecki/Minden Pictures/FLPA, (i) Mark Moffett/Minden Pictures/FLPA
Ostrich (m) Michael Krabs/Photolibrary.com, (i) Jurgen & Christine Sohns/FLPA
Cheetah (m) Winfried Wisniewski/FN/Minden/FLPA, (i) Richard Du Toit/naturepl.com
Sperm whale (m) Brandon Cole/naturepl.com, (i) Flip Nicklin/Minden Pictures/FLPA
Spectacled fruit bat (m) Theo Allofs/Minden Pictures/FLPA
Arctic tern (m) Winfried Wisniewski/Minden Pictures/FLPA
Japanese macaque (m) Ingo Arndt/naturepl.com, (i) Dickie Duckett/FLPA
Lesser flamingo (m) Anup Shah/naturepl.com, (i) Anup Shah/naturepl.com
Star-nosed mole (m) Dembinsky Photo Ass./FLPA, (i) Breck P Kent/Photolibrary.com
Galapagos marine iguana (m) Tui De Roy/Minden Pictures/FLPA, (i) Michio Hoshino/Minden Pictures/FLPA
Steller's sea eagle (m) Sergey Gorshkov/Minden Pictures/FLPA, (i) Kerstin Hinze/naturepl.com
Pale-throated sloth (m) Staffan Widstrand/naturepl.com

Every effort has been made to acknowledge the source and copyright holder of each picture.
Miles Kelly Publishing apologizes for any unintentional errors or omissions.

Made with paper from a sustainable forest

www.mileskelly.net info@mileskelly.net

CONTENTS

GET AHEAD: PUSHING THE LIMITS

The giant red centipede has dozens of legs and poison fangs – but fewer hiding places than its smaller cousins.

Out in the wild, danger lurks behind every tree, leaf, rock and ledge, and in any dark corner. The natural world is extremely perilous, so it pays to be extreme too. Being not just slightly better than the rest, but way out ahead, brings more chance of survival.

However, going to extremes does have its problems. Really massive creatures may be powerful, but they are also huge, slow targets for predators. Animals that have adapted to thrive in the harshest conditions might not cope if these conditions change. Like the rest of nature, it's a continual balancing act to be extreme, but not excessive.

There is no bigger fish than the whale shark, yet it can be attacked by a group of predators, such as dolphins, killer whales or other sharks.

1

NONE BIGGER

SIZE MATTERS
Bigger is better, up to a point. More muscle and bulk may make you a heavyweight champion. But gigantic animals can only live in places where food is plentiful and there is enough space to move around.

← Springboks leap and bounce to show predators how speedy they are and that there's no point chasing them.

SUPER SPRINGY

4 SPEED THRILLS

Extreme speed is best for escaping enemies and chasing prey. However a sudden burst of energy cannot last long, and it puts great strain on the body. Then a slower enemy with more stamina might catch you up, or your prey may find the strength to outrun you.

↓ No other creatures can stand the icy conditions of the emperor penguin breeding ground. The extreme cold even claims some penguin lives.

3 WEAPONS

Teeth, claws, beaks, tails, spines – long and sharp are best. If there's poison as well, even better. Just make sure these body parts aren't damaged. Otherwise there is no way to attack, and no defence either.

FIERCE FANGS

THE BIG FREEZE

2 CONDITIONS

Extremophiles are creatures that thrive in severe conditions – boiling hot, freezing cold, extra-dry, even too salty. But this only works if other extremophiles live there too, otherwise there's no food.

↑ The two-striped forest pit-viper sometimes pretends to bite or strike to scare enemies away – saving its venom for later.

Famed as the fastest fish in the sea, the sailfish is an open-ocean hunter of smaller shoaling fish such as mackerel and anchovies. Where these gather, so do loose groups of sailfish. They circle the prey at extreme speed, forcing them into a tight rounded bunch know as a baitball. If the prey start to scatter, the sailfish suddenly erect their folded fins to frighten them back into the ball. Then the sailfish dash at the ball to stun and gobble up the quarry.

SPRINTER SAILOR

NO WAY OUT ...

Like wolves circling deer, sailfish drive their food into a compact clump, so greatly increasing the chances of capture.

SPECIAL FEATURES

TAIL: The caudal fin (tail) is slim, stiff and crescent-shaped – the perfect shape for speedy swimming with limited manoeuvrability.

SAIL DOWN: Usually the dorsal fin or sail, which is held up by long, bony fin rays (rods), is folded down along the top or upper side of the body.

Sailfish

Scientific name: *Istiophorus albicans* (Atlantic sailfish)
Type: Fish
Lifespan: 4–5 years
Length: 3 m
Weight: 60–70 kg
Range: Atlantic, Caribbean
Status: Not assessed

SWIPE...

The long, pointed snout is known as the bill. The sailfish uses its bill to jab at fish in the baitball as it swims past. Then it rushes back in to swallow them whole.

STAR FACT

Estimates for sailfish speed vary, but the upper limits are thought to be in the region of 100–110 km/h, which is about the same as the cheetah on land.

SAIL UP: When the sailfish quickly extends its massive dorsal fin, smaller fish are scared into a panic, making them easier to target.

BILL: Apart from being a hunting weapon, the sword-like bill is also used in self defence against sharks and killer whales, and is excellent for streamlining.

As the world's tallest animal, the giraffe has several advantages over other African bush plant-eaters. It can reach leaves higher in trees, see farther for approaching danger, and lope along at a seemingly leisurely gallop that soon leaves other creatures far behind. But there are drawbacks too. Eating low plants and drinking mean awkward stooping and great effort. Mating is tricky and ungainly. And when a baby giraffe is born, it's in for quite a fall.

HIGHEST LIFE

GO LOW ...

A giraffe must splay its front legs widely in order to bend its shoulders and neck enough to drink at the waterhole.

STAR FACT

The giraffe's neck is as long as a human adult is tall. Yet inside it are just seven neck bones – the same number as there are in the necks of humans and other mammals.

SPECIAL FEATURES

NECK: Apart from extra-high feeding, the heavy, muscular neck can be swung around like a battering ram to bash rivals or predators.

HOOVES: The giraffe can strike out surprisingly suddenly and reach a long way with its sharp-edged hooves, which are as wide as dinner plates.

Giraffe

Scientific name: *Giraffa camelopardalis*
Type: Mammal
Lifespan: 20–25 years
Height: Male 5.5 m, female 4.5 m
Weight: Male 1.4 tonnes, female 800 kg
Range: Mainly east and southern Africa
Status: Least concern

LOOK...

Everything about the giraffe is extremely elongated, including its face and nose, which give added reach when browsing tree-tops.

MOUTH AND LIPS: Thick, tough skin around the lips and mouth mean that the giraffe is rarely bothered by prickly plants, even sharp-thorned acacia trees.

TONGUE: Extending the exceptionally long, flexible, grasping tongue adds another 50 cm to the giraffe's feeding height.

Supreme aerial hunter, the peregrine falcon preys mainly on fellow fliers. Its diet includes medium-sized birds from starlings to pigeons, plus the occasional bat, and ground-dwellers such as voles, rats, squirrels and young rabbits. Famed for its extreme speed when diving, the peregrine seemingly streaks down from nowhere to slam into its quarry with its sharp talons (claws), which then pierce and clasp the stunned victim.

AIR ACE KILLER

STAR FACT

The peregrine is the world's most widespread bird of prey. Despite its speed and agility in the air, it can fall victim to its larger cousins such as the golden eagle and eagle owl.

ON GUARD...

Peregrines nest on the ledges of cliffs and man-made structures such as bridges and skyscrapers. The mother guards the chicks at the nest as the male brings them food.

SPECIAL FEATURES

WINGS: The peregrine's wings are broad and back-swept, tapering to a point at the tip – the best design for speed and aerobatic manoeuvres.

TALONS: The powerful talons close on prey with a strong grip and hold it while the peregrine plucks and dismembers it.

Peregrine falcon

Scientific name: *Falco peregrinus*
Type: Bird
Lifespan: 15–20 years
Length: Male 45 cm, female 55 cm
Weight: Male 0.7 kg, female 1.2 kg
Range: Worldwide except polar regions, New Zealand
Status: Least concern

PREPARE TO DIVE...

As a peregrine enters its power-dive or 'stoop' to attack a lower-flying bird victim, it becomes the fastest of all animals, reaching speeds of more than 340 km/h.

BILL: Typically hooked and sharp-tipped for ripping flesh, the bill also has a small notch in the upper part to cut or break the neck of its prey.

EYESIGHT: Huge eyes mean the high-flying peregrine can spot fast-moving prey from above, against the backdrop of the ground below.

In tip-top breeding condition, ready to dominate his patch of beach, the elephant seal can be one of nature's truly awesome sights. With his massive rearing bulk and fearsome, ear-splitting roars, he challenges other males who try to take over his batch of females. The name 'elephant' comes mainly from this seal's long, floppy nose, but it could be from his enormous size. In best seasonal condition a well-fed male can tip the scales at 4 tonnes, which is as heavy as a real elephant.

BEACH MASTER

'STAR FACT

Elephant seals come ashore for between two and three months to breed, but they spend the rest of the year in the deep, cold ocean.

The vast dominant males, called alphas or 'beachmasters', defend their territories in vicious fights in which they push, clash and bite for hours.

FIGHT...

SPECIAL FEATURES

SIZE: The male's huge, heavyweight body helps when battling rival males at breeding time. Only the winners will mate with the females.

PROTECTION: A thick layer of blubber (fat) under the skin retains body warmth in cold seas and protects against the slashing teeth of rivals.

Elephant seal

Scientific name: *Mirounga leonina*
(Southern elephant seal)
Type: Mammal
Lifespan: Male 20 years, female 25 years
Length: Male 6 m, female 3 m
Weight: Male up to 5 tonnes, female 650 kg
Range: Southern oceans, seas and islands
Status: Least concern

MOVE IT ...

Other wildlife, such as king penguins, keep a safe distance as a male elephant seal prepares to take over a patch of beach.

DIVING: In extreme cases the elephant seal can hold its breath for two hours as it dives to depths of more than 1000 m to hunt for food.

FEEDING: Squid and fish are the main items on the elephant seal's menu, but it can also crunch up crabs, lobsters and shellfish such as clams.

Hmmm, bzzzz, mmmm ... a hummingbird's special humming sound comes from its wings, which in some species beat up to 100 times each second. This fast flapping allows the tiny bird to hover like a helicopter, and even fly sideways and backwards. But such an energy-intensive way of moving means that hummingbirds are constantly in need of food, chiefly sugary plant saps and flower nectar.

HURRIED HUMMER

A hovering hummingbird holds its main body vertical (upright) so that its wings push air almost straight downwards. Faster flapping means that it will rise straight upwards.

HOVER...

SPECIAL FEATURES

WINGS: The slim, triangular, pointed wings are excellent for speedy flaps, although the design is poor for gliding and soaring.

SIGHT: The hummingbird's colour vision is acute, allowing it to pick out suitable nectar-rich flowers as well as catch the occasional bug or spider.

Black-throated hummingbird

Scientific name: *Anthracothorax nigricollis* and others
Type: Bird
Lifespan: 5–7 years
Length: 10 cm
Weight: 7 g
Range: South America
Status: Least concern

STAR FACT

Some types of hummingbird make long migrations (seasonal journeys), covering distances of more than 3000 km. The human equivalent would be halfway to the Moon!

ME, ME...

Courting female (left) and male black-throated mango hummingbirds swoop, dive, hover and peck imaginary blooms, as each tries to impress the other.

BEAK: The extremely long, thin, slightly down-curved beak is the best shape for probing deeply into the middle of flowers.

TONGUE: The lengthy tongue laps nectar and also tastes its sugar content, so the bird does not waste time feeding at flowers where nectar is thin and diluted.

Probably the most poisonous fish in the sea, the stonefish could also win the title of the ugliest. But its tubby body, lumpy skin, strange fins and mottled colours are ideal camouflage among reefs and rocks in the shallows. Here this ambush predator waits, lying quite still, until a smaller fish, shrimp or similar creature swims by. Then with a sudden lunge the stonefish open its huge mouth and sucks in the meal.

DEADLY VENOM

Stonefish

Scientific name: Synanceia (several species)
Type: Fish
Lifespan: Not known, perhaps 10 years
Length: 40 cm
Range: Shallow tropical seas of Pacific and Indian Ocean
Status: Not enough information

People paddling in the shallows may not see a half-buried stonefish until they step on its poison spines and feel the first waves of stinging pain.

OUCH ...

'STAR FACT

Stonefish are tough survivors, with thick, leathery skin to resist wounds from sharp rocks and sea urchin spines.

SPECIAL FEATURES

EYES AND MOUTH: The eyes and mouth are on top of the head facing upwards, so the stonefish can keep a constant watch on prey passing above.

VENOM: Thirteen short, sharp spines on the fish's back pierce and inject venom into any creature that tries to attack.

Sunfish

Scientific name: Mola mola
Type: Fish
Lifespan: 10–12 years
Height: 3 m
Weight: Up to 1.5 tonnes
Range: Worldwide except cold and polar seas
Status: Not assessed

SUN BATHER

Despite eating mainly jellyfish, squid and similar soft-bodied creatures, the ocean sunfish grows to be the world's largest bony fish. (This group includes all fish with bony skeletons – not cartilage-skeleton sharks.) After diving deep into colder water to feed, the sunfish lives up to its name by lying on its side at the water's surface to soak up the warmth of the Sun's rays.

LET'S GO...

Lacking a proper tail, the sunfish 'rows' along by waving its dorsal (upper) and anal (lower) fins from side to side like oars.

STAR FACT

The adult sunfish's extreme size makes it too big for most ocean predators, except large sharks and killer whales.

SPECIAL FEATURES

SKIN: The tough skin is up to 6 cm thick and is covered by tiny tooth-like denticles rather than the usual scales.

MOUTH: The sunfish's teeth are fused (joined) into a strong 'beak' that is suited to cutting up both floppy, squidgy jellyfish and hard shellfish.

No other creatures can survive the conditions that emperor penguins endure. Huddled in an Antarctic gale, they face stinging snow and wind-chill of −50°C. These flightless fish-hunters waddle more than 80 kilometres inland to their breeding site. After mating, the females return to the ocean to hunt, while the males stand together, each keeping an egg warm on his feet. Nine weeks pass before the chick hatches and the well-fed female returns to take over the care.

BLIZZARD BIRD

Emperor penguin

Scientific name: *Aptenodytes forsteri*
Type: Bird
Lifespan: 20–25 years, rarely 40-plus
Height: 1.2 m
Weight: 30–40 kg
Range: Antarctica
Status: Least concern

'STAR FACT

Over the course of the journey inland, courtship, caring for the egg and chick, and finally travelling back to the sea to feed, the male's body weight may decrease by 50 percent, from 40 to 20 kg.

SHIVER...

After the females leave, the males gather in close groups to share body warmth. They take turns braving the outside and sheltering on the inside.

SPECIAL FEATURES

WARMTH: The penguin's copious layers of feathers keep its body at a snug 39°C, helped by a 3-cm-thick fatty layer of blubber under the skin.

HUDDLING: The temperature in the middle of an emperor penguin huddle can be more than 70°C higher than on the outer edge.

COOL...

The chick is secure on the father's leathery, non-slip feet, sheltered by a flap of blubbery skin and feathers hanging down from his belly, called the brood pouch.

VOCAL CALLS: A courting couple call loudly to each other. When the female returns from the sea, nine weeks after laying, she locates her mate by calling for him.

DIVING: When the penguins return to the sea they hunt, diving for 20 minutes at a time to depths of 500 m to restock their body food reserves with fish.

Army ant colonies are constantly on the move, marching along tropical forest floors. All the ants within the colony serve the lead ant – the queen – and do different jobs to ensure the colony's survival. Army ants have no permanent home – at night they form a temporary shelter (bivouac) out of their own bodies to protect the queen and her larvae (young). Any small creatures that stray into the colony's path, such as beetles, other ants, mice, lizards and baby birds, are bitten and stung to death, torn into bits and eaten.

FOOT SOLDIER

YUM...

Workers cut up and carry pieces of food back to the main colony for the larvae, soldiers and queen.

SPECIAL FEATURES

NUMBERS: Small army ant colonies number a few thousand, but a big group may have more than one million individuals.

SWARMING: If a few ants find food or get into a fight, they release chemical messages called pheromones. In seconds, thousands come to help.

Army ant

Scientific name: *Eciton* and others
Type: Insect
Lifespan: Workers 3–12 months, queens 10-plus years
Length: Workers 5–10 mm, soldiers 20-plus mm
Range: Most tropical regions
Status: Least concern

ATTACK...

A soldier ant's extremely long, curved, pointed jaws (visible just below the feelers) are called mandibles, and work like stabbing pincers.

STAR FACT

Soldier army ants have such outsized mouthparts that they cannot feed themselves, so the worker ants do this chore.

FEARLESSNESS: The soldiers act by instinct and have no fear. They have no problem attacking enemies that are thousands of times larger than themselves.

DIGESTION: Powerful chemicals in the ant's venom and digestive system can dissolve almost any part of any animal victim, even horns and hooves.

A champion of extremes for many reasons, the ostrich is the tallest, heaviest and fastest-running of all birds. It also lays the biggest eggs and may have the widest diet. Plant foods such as leaves, grasses, shoots, seeds and fruits are its mainstay. But a hungry ostrich snaps up worms, spiders and insects such as beetles and locusts as well as scavenging, vulture-like, on the kills of predators such as lions and hyaenas.

BIGGEST BIRDIE

KEEPING WATCH...

The grey-brown female keeps her eggs warm and guarded by day, well camouflaged against dry plants and earth. At night the black-feathered male takes over.

SPECIAL FEATURES

FEET: The huge feet have only two toes each, compared to four on most other birds. The inner toe has a formidable claw for slashing enemies.

LEGS: The leg design is typical of a speedy mover, with most of the muscle bulk high in the hip region, and a very long shin.

Ostrich

Scientific name: *Struthio camelus*
Type: Bird
Lifespan: 40 years, rarely more
Height: 2–2.2 m
Weight: Up to 140 kg
Range: Africa south of the Sahara
Status: Least concern

STAR FACT

The ostrich egg is the world's biggest, at 15 cm long and 13 cm wide, and weighing 1.5 kg. Yet it is one of the smallest eggs in proportion to the body size of the bird that lays it.

RUN ...

A panicked ostrich can reach speeds of more than 70 km/h as it tries to escape danger – and can keep running for an hour or more.

GUTS: The ostrich swallows up to one kg of pebbles into its first gut compartment, the muscular gizzard, to helps its digestive system grind up tough plant matter.

SIGHT: Huge eyes, each 5 cm across, allow the ostrich to see extreme details both at a distance and up close.

A young springbok raises its head to sniff and look around — and sees a cheetah rocketing towards it. This big cat must catch its quarry within 30 seconds, or its body will overheat from the extreme effort required to bound along faster than any other land animal. The springbok tries to zig-zag but the cheetah responds, swishing its tail from side to side to aid its sudden fast turns. The cheetah rapidly bowls over the springbok, clamps its jaws onto the victim's windpipe, and waits for its struggle to subside.

SPRINT CHAMP

When it is within striking distance the cheetah extends a front leg and hooks a claw into its prey to trip it up.

GOTCHA...

'STAR FACT

'Tear stripes' — thin black lines that extend from the inside of each eye to the corner of the mouth — may work like anti-glare sunglasses to help the cheetah see in the fierce midday sun.

SPECIAL FEATURES

BUILD: The cheetah is slim, lightweight and long-legged. Most of its muscle bulk is in the shoulders and hips, to move its limbs.

FLEXIBILITY: The bendy backbone arches up as the cheetah's legs extend front and rear, then curves down as the legs come together under it.

Cheetah

Scientific name: *Acinonyx jubatus*
Type: Mammal
Lifespan: 10–12 years
Length: Head-body 1.2 m, tail 80 cm
Weight: 40–60 kg
Range: North, east and southern Africa
Status: Vulnerable

LAUNCH...

Hurling itself from the cover of a bush, the cheetah lowers its small head for extra streamlining, extends its claws for a better grip on the ground, and the race is on.

ACCELERATION: From standstill to 100 km/h takes a cheetah just three seconds, an incredible rate that few prey animals can match.

TOP SPEED: Cheetahs have been clocked running at speeds of more than 100 km/h, and in very short bursts as fast as 120 km/h.

Forget the lion, tiger, bear, great white and killer whale – the world's largest predator by far is the sperm whale, and it is heavier than all those others combined. This massive monster has titanic deep-sea battles with its prey, the world's largest invertebrate, the giant squid. The sperm whale holds other records too: it has the world's biggest brain, at 8 kilograms (six times bigger than our own), and it undertakes the longest, deepest dives of any air-breathing animal.

GIANT HUNTER

TIME TO DIVE...

Raising its massive tail flukes above the surface means that the sperm whale is about to head straight down into the blackness of the ocean depths.

SPECIAL FEATURES

DIVING: This whale's muscles and blood have many more microscopic oxygen-storing cells and substances than those found in other animals.

BREATHING: At the surface, the whale takes a huge breath every 10–12 seconds. Breathing out sends a steamy fountain 15 m into the air.

Sperm whale

Scientific name: *Physeter macrocephalus*
Type: Mammal
Lifespan: 60–70 years
Length: Male 20 m, female 13 m
Weight: Male 50 tonnes, female 20 tonnes
Range: All oceans
Status: Vulnerable

BIG HEAD ...

The whale's huge forehead is mostly full of a waxy oil known as spermaceti. This may alter the animal's buoyancy (ability to float), helping it to descend and then return to the surface.

STAR FACT

By tracking individual sperm whales, scientists have learnt that these mammals can dive below 3000 m and stay underwater for 90 minutes.

TEETH: The teeth are only visible in the lower jaw, with about 20–25 on each side. In the upper jaw they are small and remain below the gum surface.

FOREHEAD: The spermaceti in the head may also help to focus sound waves, which might play a part in the whale's echolocation navigation system.

As dusk falls in the rainforest, it's time for the fruit bat colony to wake up, yawn and groom themselves with claws and teeth. They flap along from their daytime roost to the feeding area, which could be as far as 70 kilometres away, on their extremely long wings. Here they cluster around the latest ripe fruits and begin to lick, nibble, suck and chew to extract the soft pulp and juices, then spit out the hard, stringy bits.

FRUITY FLAPPER

Spectacled fruit bat

Scientific name: *Pteropus conspicillatus*
Type: Mammal
Lifespan: 12–15 years
Length: Male 25 cm, female 22 cm
Weight: Male 900 g, female 700 g
Range: New Guinea, northeast Australia
Status: Least concern

WOW...

A lever mechanism in the bat's foot bones means that when it hangs, its toes automatically curl around so that it grips the perch with hardly any effort.

'STAR FACT

The fruit bat's long muzzle, used for smelling ripe fruits, and big ears, give it the common name of flying fox.

SPECIAL FEATURES

SIGHT: Big, sensitive eyes mean the spectacled fruit bat can see well to fly and feed in the dark, except on cloudy, moonless nights.

WINGS: With a span of more than 110 cm, the wings are held out by extremely long, thin finger bones. The claw is the thumb.

ETERNAL FLIER

The Arctic tern is the world's greatest animal traveller, and never sees winter. It breeds in the far north around the Arctic during summer, then spends three months flying from the top to the bottom of the world, arriving at the far south of Antarctica – where it is also summer. After a few months of rest and refuelling, it's time to complete its giant round trip and return to the Arctic, and the cycle starts all over again.

'STAR FACT

Each migration may be 20,000 km. A lifetime of lengthy flights means an Arctic tern may travel a distance equivalent to a return journey to the Moon.

Arctic tern

Scientific name: *Sterna paradisaea*
Type: Bird
Lifespan: 25–30 years
Length: 35 cm
Weight: 110 g
Range: Arctic and Antarctic (migrates between the two)
Status: Least concern

KEEP OUT...

Arctic terns defend their nests by diving at intruders, calling loudly and even swooping down to peck, or release foul-smelling fluids.

SPECIAL FEATURES

STAMINA: This tern's extraordinary migration takes from two to four months, snatching quick snacks from the ocean surface along the route.

BEAK: The tern flutters and then dips down to the surface or even plunges in, to grasp fish with its long, slim, ridge-edged beak.

In the depths of winter, when snow carpets the ground and lakes freeze solid, relaxing in a hot tub might seem a human luxury. But the macaques of Japan, sometimes called 'snow monkeys', have taken to bathing in the natural hot springs scattered across the country. These are the most northern-dwelling of all monkeys and apes (apart from humans), and they cope with extremes of temperature as low as –15°C in winter and up to 30°C in summer.

SNOWY SPA BATHER

CLEVER...

Parent macaques teach their young how to feed, bathe, and generally survive during an extended infancy of more than two years.

SPECIAL FEATURES

DIET: The macaque's foods changes with the seasons, from bark and buds in winter, to shoots and flowers in spring, then fruits in autumn.

HANDS: The monkey's thumb is opposable, like our own, able to grip and manipulate foods and other objects very precisely.

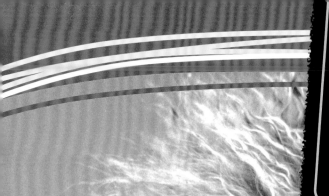

Japanese macaque

Scientific name: *Macaca fuscata*
Type: Mammal
Lifespan: 25–30 years
Length: Head-body 70 cm, tail 10 cm
Weight: Males up to 12 kg, females up to 9 kg
Range: Islands of Japan
Status: Least concern

'STAR FACT

In some troops of Japanese macaques, the monkeys have been observed pressing snow into balls with their hands, then rolling the snowball along to make it larger – seemingly just for fun.

ME FIRST ...

In macaque troops, females outnumber males and have a hierarchy, or pecking order, showing who is boss. The chief or dominant individuals get first choice of the best places in the hot spring.

FUR: The macaque's warm fur coat grows even thicker in winter to protect it from the worst of the winds, rain and snow in their upland habitats.

INTELLIGENCE: The clever Japanese macaque quickly picks up new tricks, and has learnt to wash sand or mud off its food before eating.

A constant hubbub of low squawks, grunts and even cow-like mooing make the flamingo nesting colony a busy place. Thousands of these tall, long-necked, stilt-legged wading birds arrive, leave and jostle for space among the volcano-like mounds of mud that are their nests. Some of the lakes where lesser flamingoes set up colonies are so hot and caustic (salty) that they would burn human skin. But the unconcerned birds wade easily and feed hungrily, stopping occasionally to preen their pink plumage.

SALTY SURVIVOR

The newly hatched chick has stumpy legs and a short, straight beak. It does not gain its spindly adult proportions until it is one year old.

CUTE ...

SPECIAL FEATURES

LEGS: The flamingo has the extremely long, thin legs of a wading bird, allowing it to walk safely in water more than 40 cm deep.

FEET: The bird's wide-toed webbed feet are ideal for walking on soft mud or sand. The tough skin resists water temperatures of more than 40°C.

AWESOME...

Colonies of more than two million lesser flamingoes crowd the highly salty lakes of east Africa.

Lesser flamingo

Scientific name: *Phoenicopterus minor*
Type: Bird
Lifespan: Up to 50 years
Height: 90–100 cm
Weight: 2 kg
Range: Africa, southern Asia
Status: Near threatened

'STAR FACT

The flamingo feeds on tiny, plant-like life-forms called blue-green algae. The algae provide substances that the bird alters within its body to give its feathers their pink colour.

NECK: Long legs raise the body up high, but the equally elongated neck compensates so the bird can easily reach down to its foot level to feed.

BILL: The deep, angled beak has rows of comb-like ridges inside. These work as filters to strain tiny plants, and also small shrimps and worms, from the water.

Snuffle, probe, feel, catch, bite, swallow! In less than half a second the star-nosed mole can locate, identify and eat a small prey item. This mini-mole, which could fit in an adult's hand, is an expert predator both underground and underwater. It gobbles up any small creatures, including worms, bugs, tadpoles, small fish, shrimps and little shellfish. Its star feature is its star-shaped nose, which is extremely sensitive to touch and taste as well as smell.

STARRY SWIMMER

'STAR FACT

The star organ is a ring of 22 fleshy, bendy, finger-like tentacles, its total size about as wide as your fingernail. Each tentacle can move on its own to touch and feel with incredible accuracy.

QUICK ...

The multi-purpose front feet are spades for digging in earth, paddles for swimming and levers for moving underwater rocks to find prey.

SPECIAL FEATURES

FUR: The thick double-coat of fur repels water so the mole does not get waterlogged and cold on its underwater expeditions.

SMELL: Underwater, the mole can breathe bubbles of air out of its nose onto interesting objects, then breathe them in again to detect any smell.

Star-nosed mole

Scientific name: *Condylura cristata*
Type: Mammal
Lifespan: 2–4 years
Length: Up to 20 cm
Weight: 50 g
Range: Eastern North America
Status: Least concern

HUNGRY...

The star-nosed mole is on the go day and night, needing big meals every few hours. It must eat enough to keep its little body warm and fuel its hyperactive lifestyle.

FRONT FEET: Like most moles, this species uses its powerful, massive-clawed front feet to dig burrows, both to live in and when foraging for food.

TAIL: During times of plentiful food the mole's tail grows thicker with stored fat, which is used later as an energy reserve when prey is scarce.

Marine iguanas are found only on the Galapagos Islands. They are also the only lizards that regularly dive into salty water, and the only reptiles to eat just seaweeds and similar plants. Although they lie on the Equator, the seas around the Galapagos are surprisingly chilly, at 22–24°C. After each dive for food, the iguana must sit on a seaside rock to warm itself before it can venture back into the cool water. Each lizard has its own favoured patch of rock as its territory, which it jealously defends against intruders.

SEAWEED EATER

STAR FACT

Special glands in the iguana's nose collect unwanted salt from its food. The lizard then sneezes out the salt, which often ends up as a pile of white crystals on its head.

SPECIAL FEATURES

DIVING: Marine iguanas can dive to depths of 15 m, lasting for 30 minutes on one breath of air. Deeper than this the water is too cold and dark.

SNOUT: Its short, blunt snout allows the marine iguana to scrape off the newest, most nutritious seaweeds or algae coating the rocks.

SCRAPE...

The iguana nibbles fresh seaweed growths from the submerged rocks using its small but very sharp teeth.

Galapagos marine iguana

Scientific name: *Amblyrhynchus cristatus*
Type: Reptile
Lifespan: 20 years
Length: Male up to 1.5 m, female 1 m
Weight: 1–2 kg
Range: Galapagos Islands (Pacific Ocean)
Status: Vulnerable

BEWARE...

When iguanas first emerge from the sea they are so cold that they cannot run away if threatened, so they are very ready to bite enemies.

CLAWS: The iguana's claws are long, curved and sharp, to grip slippery rocks both when feeding under the surface and clambering over them when above.

TAIL: The long tail is both tall and narrow from side to side, like that of a crocodile – ideal for powerful swimming when the iguana swishes it from side to side.

Competing with the harpy and Philippine eagles as the biggest of the raptors, a well-fed female Steller's sea eagle can be heavier than either of them. With a wingspan of up to 1.3 metres, she is larger than the male – a feature seen in many birds of prey. The extremely large, fiercely hooked beak is ideal for tearing up the eagle's main prey of salmon and similar fish. In cold winters, sea and lake ice may drive the eagle inland to hunt rabbits, lemmings and smaller birds.

FISHY RAPTOR

STAR FACT

Far from being a noble hunter, this eagle may be a sneaky kleptoparasite (a creature that robs other animals of their meals). It chases and attacks other birds, forces them to drop or cough up any food they have, and then it eats it.

SWOOP ...

The sea eagle circles several metres above the water's surface, scanning for signs of fish below such as ripples, bubbles, shadowy movements or exposed fins.

SPECIAL FEATURES

SIZE: The largest aerial hunter in its region, an adult Steller's sea eagle is too big to be attacked by other birds, or by many mammals either.

FEET: The long, scale-covered toes and extremely sharp talons are adapted for gripping slippery, slimy, struggling fish.

Steller's sea eagle

Scientific name: *Haliaeetus pelagicus*
Type: Bird
Lifespan: 20–25 years
Length: Male 90 cm, female 100 cm
Weight: Male 5 kg, female 8 kg
Range: Coasts on northeast Asia
Status: Vulnerable

MINE...

Apart from the breeding season, Steller's sea eagles usually live and hunt alone. If food is scarce they may gather at a source such as a whale carcass and fight over the remains.

BEAK: The typical bird-of-prey hooked beak has exceptionally sharp edges and a tightly curved tip, suited to slicing through a fish's scaly skin.

FEATHERS: The sea eagle's home area has long, cold winters, so the bird's plumage is extra-thick with very fluffy down feathers under the outer layer.

Almost everything about the pale-throated three-toed sloth is slow in the extreme. Its movements are unhurried and deliberate. It chews at a very leisurely pace. Its digestive system dawdles along, taking many days to digest each leafy meal. Its waste disposal is also sluggish, with droppings produced only once each week. However a frightened sloth can strike out surprisingly fast with its large, powerful claws, to inflict serious wounds on enemies.

SLOWLY DOES IT

YAWN ...

Sloths either rest, doze or sleep for up to 18 hours each day. They are able to hang on in their treetop homes even when deeply asleep.

Pale-throated sloth

Scientific name: *Bradypus tridactylus*
Type: Mammal
Lifespan: 12–15 years
Length: 50 cm
Weight: 4 kg
Range: Forests of Central and South America
Status: Least concern

STAR FACT

Unlike other mammals, sloths allow their body temperature to vary with their surroundings. When it gets cold, they get even slower!

SPECIAL FEATURES

CLIMBING Three long claws on each foot dig deep into bark, allowing the sloth to cling securely to a trunk or hang upside down from a bough.

CAMOUFLAGE: Tiny plants and mosses grow in grooves and pits in the sloth's fur, giving it extremely accurate camouflage.